MW01063594

I WROTE YOU
A POEM

(I WROTE YOU EVERY POEM)

Kristina Mahr

For anyone who needs to read these words.

And for me, who needed to write them.

A NOTE

These poems are arranged chronologically and written
over a six-month span.

I call them the aftermath of the aftermath.

What happens when the blood is gone and all you're left
with is scar tissue.

Scar tissue and memories and hands that do not know,
have not yet learned, how to let go.

But they are trying.

That's What I Wanted To Tell You

You say the past can't hurt me,
and I wonder why it is
that my memories come with daggers
when yours don't.

I guess I paid extra for these.

(In blood, in tears.)

I've thought about this,
the things I want to tell you,
the way I want to tell you.
I've thought about this –
about how my heart weighs more now,
and how it used to drag me
oceans deep,
but I learned to swim,
or, I guess,
I learned to drown
without the burning.

If my heart weighs more now,
it's because you filled it.

That's what I wanted to tell you.

Spin Me

Spin me –
I'm tired of being the one who stands still.
You found me
when I didn't even know
I was lost
and then you lost me
somewhere
where nobody else could find me.
Remember the way
I looked for you?
Now it's the way
I look
for me.

I Just Don't Know

I just don't know
how one goes about
not wanting you
in that big way,
in that way that gapes
like a cut throat,
like a forced smile,
like a door
held open
against hands that try to slam it.
It's a hell of a thing,
but I just don't know
how one goes about
not wanting you.

I Won't

I won't lie to you.
I have,
and I could,
but I won't.
I made scrapbooks
of my scars,
and I show them to you
without even bothering
to clear away the blood.
Without letting you cover
your eyes.
I turn it into a slideshow.
I project it on the clouds.
Look, is what I want to say.
Look, I have been hurt.
And look.
Look, I'm trying here,
I'm trying here
and there and everywhere,
in the very depths
of me,
I'm trying here –
to not be afraid
that it'll happen
all over
again.

You

Keep me,
but like how we keep
the sunshine of the day before
on our skin
in the middle of the night.
(As a memory.)
Maybe as a promise, too,
if we could ever find a way
to promise
that the sun will rise again.
I just want there to be
a single goddamn thing in this world
that I can count on.
I just want that thing
to be you.

What I Am

What am I?
I'm a struggle
covered in skin.
A howl,
a feast.
I'm the moment
before the first
lightning flash,
the breath before
the sky
erupts.
I'm every little thing
you thought you wanted
before you realized
what I really was.
I'm all of it,
I'm none of it,
I'm the lantern
lost souls use
to find their way
out of dark tunnels,
the lantern
that's dropped
to the ground
the second
they're free.
(I'm waiting
for someone else
to need me.)

It Knew

Hold onto me.
(I mean it.)
I was built from
friction
and flight,
and I'm going to try
to run.
Sometimes I think about the fact that
you are the only one
who will ever be able to say
you had my heart
when it was whole.
I understand now,
what it was doing.
The way it fell in love
kicking
and
screaming.
The way it knew,
it knew,
it knew.
(It knew better.)

Shredded

I can never decide
if there was somewhere else
I was supposed to be
or someone else
I was supposed to be.
Either way,
each step I take
is both toward
and away.
I am shredded,
when I think
I was supposed to be
saved.
We're playing tag,
and you are it,
but you seem content
to stay it.
You seem content,
while I am
a scale that only ever tips,
a sea that only ever rages,
a heart,
a heart,
that only
ever
pounds.

Worth the Risk

The flowers aren't blooming yet.
They still don't trust
that winter's really gone.
Is it worth the risk?
Is any of it worth the risk,
when things end
so suddenly
and hands open
so easily
and somewhere,
there is someone
who keeps all of the right words
in his back pocket
when he knows how to fold them
into a life vest,
into a buoy,
into a whole goddamn boat –
when he knows,
but still,
he decides
to let
me drown.

Ghosts

They keep reaching for me,
even as I bat their hands away.

Maybe it's because
I also beg them to come closer.

I'm so much of a push and a pull outside,
I'm so much of the same inside.

I live with ghosts.

(I won't let them leave.)

Heartbreak

I think the world is swimming more
in heartbreak
than in ocean water.

I search faces for it.

I look for shatters
behind smiles,
wounds that needed stitches
wrapped in bandages instead.

(Because it's the best that they could do.)

(We're all doing the best that we can do.)

Memories

I want to call you up some nights
just to compare memories,
just to exchange them,
just to see if there are any you have
that I'm missing.
I know my collection is incomplete,
but the ones I have are invaluable.
The ones I have are those rare pieces
some people search for their whole lives.
I wonder which ones you have.
I wonder if any of them
are the same as mine.
I wonder if there are any
you lock away in a safe
and only look at when you're lonely.
I wonder if there are any
that make you want to
call me up some nights
to see if we can't make more.

A Weakness

I have a weakness, still,
for you,
in a hard shift,
in a dizzying change,
like the earth is all the same,
it just started spinning
the other way.
In the way loving you
was a strength
just yesterday.

I Go, Too

I know what I said,
but then I slammed my finger
in the drawer,
and instead of a curse,
I screamed your name.
(I know I said that I was fine.)
I stomp, though,
and the rafters shake,
and the birds fly away,
and nothing,
nothing,
stays.
(I go, too.)
You will see me
and think that I'm still here,
but I
go
too.

Walls

I don't know what
makes me sadder –
that the walls you've built
keep me out
or that they keep you in.

(The world would like to see you.)

(I would like to see you.)

A Beautiful Thing

I look at you
through the gaps
between my fingers
when I try
not to look at you
at all.
It is still a beautiful thing,
still a beautiful thing,
even if it's only my
beautiful thing
instead of ours –
this love,
the way I love you.
It is still
a beautiful
thing.

The Things Worth Keeping

I still lean back.
Even as my feet
carry me forward,
I lean back.
I have to keep reminding myself
that you're not back there.
If anything,
you're ahead.
You're when
we're both a little older
and both a little wiser
and both know a little better
how to hold onto
the things
worth keeping.

Cowards

Nobody leaves me better than you.
These cowards,
who back away in inches.
Who call or text
because they're weak
and miss me,
who take it back,
the fools,
who want to try again.
Nobody leaves me
better
than you.

Coming to Terms

I have come to terms with the fact that
there will always be a knot
in the middle of this necklace,
in the same way there will always be knots
in my veins and arteries,
where the blood doesn't flow quite right,
where my pulse scatters and scrambles,
where missing you has made
a mess of my insides.
I have come to terms with the fact that
we have nothing more to say,
but oh how badly
I still want
to hear
your voice.

That's All There Is

Someday someone
may find these words,
but it won't be somewhere romantic
like a bottle in the ocean
or a tin can buried under a tree.
They'll just be scratched on a pad of paper
next to my bed
or on an internet search of my name
or "love"
or "heartbreak."
I'm creating this record,
every day,
of how someone will see
what you were to me.
Here, I'll make this easier –
I loved him.
That's all there is.

Because of Me

I'm still testing
and probing
which parts of me
are glass.

(Which parts shatter.)

Which parts are rubber.

(Which parts stretch.)

Which parts are kindling.

(Which parts burn.)

I'm still testing
and probing
and learning
and discovering
who I am
and how I am
and why I am.

(Some of it's because of you.)

(The best parts are because of me.)

The Thunder

This line is crowded,
covered in things I've laid down on it.
I have to step so carefully over them all
as I walk along it.

(I didn't know my heart
    could take up so much space.)

Hey,
I just wanted to say,
there's a thunderstorm in my veins tonight,
and it's keeping me awake.

Hey,
I just wanted to say –
the thunder
sounds an awful lot
like your voice.

(I open the window.)

(I let it in.)

It Helps

I am wound too tightly
to make any sort of music.
I snap
at the slightest
touch.
It doesn't need to be this way.
There's a vase
on my dining room table
I bought
in case you ever
sent me flowers.
(It's coated in, covered in, dust.)
I still let strangers
reach inside my chest.
(I haven't learned my lesson.)
It's just that I don't always know
if anything's alive in there,
and it helps
to hear it
from them.

Good to You

Summer has a sway,
and I don't recognize you in it.
You shudder like winter,
you flourish like spring,
you wilt like fall.
You don't give
more than you're sure
you can take back.
I wanted you to sink a little,
not to slice any major arteries,
but maybe to nick a vein.
To bleed a little.
I'm covered in bandages
and scars,
and all I wanted
was a single drop
of your blood.
All I wanted
was something
in the face of my
everything.
And anyway,
this is all to say,
I hope the summer's
good to you.
I hope all of life
is good to you.
(I would've been so good to you.)

The One

Meet me in the middle
of a sunflower field
in the middle of the night.
I'll be the one
lying on my back,
counting the stars.
You'll be the one
wishing you
were somewhere else.
You'll be the one
plucking petals
one by one,
whispering you love me,
whispering you love me not.
You'll be the one,
you'll be the one.
(You'll always be the one.)

Everything

You think you're in these words?
You're in the curve of the s,
I guess,
in the lift and fall of the v.
You're in the question mark
most prominently,
and you placed yourself
in every period.
You're in the way
the words echo in my head
before I get them down on paper.
You're in the way
I press my pen down
so much harder than I need to.
You think you're in these words?
You're in everything.
Why should this be any different?

And Yet, and Still

I know everything
there is to know now,
and yet,
and still,
I just wanted to say,
I miss you.
I know every reason not to,
and yet,
and still,
I don't think
I'll ever
stop.

Finishing Touches

There's just a few more t's to cross,
just a couple more i's to dot.
That's it, that's all.
I am putting the finishing touches
on falling out of love with you.

I See a River

Let me draw you a picture
of what I see
when I close my eyes.

(I'm sorry I'm not much of an artist.)

I see you,
and I see me.
I see a river
that runs between us.
You have the boat,
I have the oars.

I'm just no longer sure
there's any such thing
as meant to be.

Conflict

I am a conflict wrapped in skin.
Did you know that about me?
There's a war being waged
amidst my bones,
a heart caught
in the crossfire.
(My heart caught in the crossfire.)
I don't know how one can contain
so many pushes and pulls,
how one sigh can be
both heartbreak and relief.
I don't know whether
this is just who I am,
or if it's who you made me.
Tell me how
your bones are at peace.
Tell me how you brokered a truce.
Tell me how you
                    surrendered.

Wrecking Ball

You agree that you're
a wrecking ball,
but
you say
a wrecking ball
can't cause any damage

unless

it's

pushed.

I Smile Like This

He asks me why I smile like this,
like it hurts,
and it stops me in my tracks
because nobody else
seems to have noticed
that my smile broke
when my heart did.

There's a drawer in my dresser
that I keep locked,
and I can tell that it bothers him.

(I never told him about you.)

It'll probably slip out some day,
in my sleep or in a scream.

In a scream in my sleep.

It'll probably slip out some day.

Until then,
I smile like this.

Gritted teeth
like prison bars
for your name.

I smile like this.

Just Another One

I don't know.
I just want to be more of a floodlight
and less of a match.
I want to blind someone,
guide someone,
not burn fingertips
and flicker out.
I don't know.
I want a lot of things.
You can trace the way
they pulse through my veins,
the way my skin can't hold them all.
You were just
another one
of those things.
I've convinced myself,
I've finally managed to convince myself –
you were just
another one
of those things.

Depth

Love is measured
in depth instead of length.
I can step over us easily,
one small step,
one little hop,
but if I fall
inside of us,
I'll drown.

Sieve

How am I?
Oh, I have
more holes in me
than I did.
I'm a little more sieve,
a little less contained,
a little less
whole,
a little more
drained.
A little more
and a little less
as one day turns into
the next.
Hold me over a garden.
Maybe something will grow
from all that I used to be.

Let Me Go

What do you do
when you're not even limbs anymore,
just fingertips,
just toes?
When you're just the ends of you.
Just the places that you stop
and something bigger than you starts.
I listened to a song today
that was only words tripping over one another,
all a rush to be said
and to be heard,
all rage fire dust blood,
and it made me want to feel
that urgently,
that fiercely.
Somebody pressed the mute button
over a year ago now –
I thought it was the pause button,
but no,
I've still been playing,
just silently.
I've still been screaming,
just silently.
I cannot tell,
I do not know,
if I need to be set back on the tracks
or allowed to finally
run off them.
(Let me go.)

Unforgivable

Tell me the things that are unforgivable.
I keep thinking I've found them,
but then I lose them.
(But then I forgive them.)
Tell me where this ends.
Does this end?
Every time I think it has,
it's only a break, only a pause.
Only a moment to inhale
before the next breath comes out rasping,
panting,
losing a race I never wanted to run.
I just wanted you to stay.
That's it, that's all.
I just wanted you to stay.

(That isn't it, that isn't all.)

(I just wanted you to love me.)

All You Do

Here I've been thinking
that I am the lighthouse
and you are the ship,
that you need me,
that this is what I'm here for,
but now I think
that I am the ship,
that I have always been the ship,
and you
are all
of the jagged
rocks.

(All you do is break me.)

Whatever's In There

I haven't unpacked my suitcase since you.
I guess I don't really need
whatever's in there,
if it's been all these months
and I haven't touched it.
I imagine I'm in there,
who I was.
(I imagine I'm screaming.)
I imagine you're in there,
who I thought you were.
(I can't hear you anymore.)
I push it under the bed.
I guess I don't really need
whatever's in there.

A Word for This

I don't think there's a word for this.
That feeling where you're on a plane
and you don't know the person next to you,
but you imagine it's him.
That feeling where your fingers flex,
your hands reach,
and you imagine he can be reached.
That feeling where the sun is setting,
and you want to lean your head on his shoulder,
and you imagine you could.
You think about trying.
You don't look to your left
because you can almost feel him there,
and the feeling will vanish
if you look.
I don't think there's a word for this.

In Peace

I dip a finger
in the future
and let it rest
on the tip of my tongue.
Still sour.
I still flicker,
I still flinch.
I shove my whole past
inside of my mouth,
and I don't know how
to swallow it.
It's sweet, though.
Like birthday cake
for someone who died
a year and some months ago.
Rest in peace,
whoever we used to be.
If I ever learn
to leave us alone,
I hope that we
rest in peace.

Pretend

I wrote you a letter
filled with things I meant to tell you
back when I thought we had more time.
Do you want to read it?
It's ok if you don't want to read it.
(It's more that I had to write it.)
Anyway, nobody takes regret
as currency these days.
I've even offered it away for free.
No takers.
I lie awake each night
with their pillow-soft weight
pressing down and down and down
across my nose and mouth.
I'm learning how one lives
when one can't always find a way to breathe.
In the mornings, I guess.
I get all of my living done in the mornings.
It's something at least.
Here, I wrote you a letter.
Pretend it says good riddance.
Pretend it says
goodbye.

Now I Wish

I never gave you thunder –
the worst you got from me
was pounding rain.

(Now I wish I'd stormed.)

(Now I wish I'd raged.)

(Now I wish I'd never let you stop loving me.)

The Only Story

I think I should start with once upon a time,
but it feels wrong without an end that's
happily ever after.

Still, there was you,
and there was me,
and that in itself feels like
once upon a time.

It feels like a fairytale
written by someone
who'd been in love
but lost.

Someone who didn't know
how to write
anything but goodbye.

Anyway, once upon a time
I loved you.

It's the only story
I've ever wanted to tell.

Don't You Think

I don't know what I thought,
but it wasn't this.
It wasn't this dip and dive,
slip and slaughter,
forgetting
and forgetting
and forgetting.
(Refusing to remember.)
I climbed mountains for you.
I was afraid, but I didn't tell you.
You see,
there is nobody here to remember.
I tell these stories,
I wait for someone to chime in,
but there is nobody here to remember.
You over there, me over here.
(Don't you think we should be remembered?)

It's Like This

I am lost,
and everyone knows it,
but they don't know
it's like this.
Like a maze with no exits
and your goodbye
in my ears.
They don't know
it's like this.

Jukebox

The jukebox keeps playing our song,
playing our song,
like it's haunted,
like it's just like me.
I don't want to hear it,
but I put the next quarter in
and I hit the same button
and I play it again.
People are dancing to it,
laughing to it,
like they haven't been pierced,
haven't sprung a leak,
aren't sinking, sinking, sinking.
I play it again,
I play it again.
My feet touch the bottom –
I could push off of it,
I could.
(I play it again.)

Better Today

I'm spinning from lampposts
and splashing in puddles
in nothing near to joy.
I am composed of
severed limbs
and rotting heartbeats,
I only laugh
to drown out my own thoughts.
I'm sorry,
I got off track,
I'm sorry –
what I meant to say
is I'm better today.
Thank you,
thank you,
for asking.

Tell Me

Tell me how I live within your memories.
Do I live well?
Do I laugh often?
Do I make you laugh often?
Are there tears in there?
(If there aren't, I wonder what you did with them.)
Am I pretty in them,
do I shine in them,
do I want too much in them?
Is there an alley where you kiss me,
a couch where you trace the curve of my ear,
do you pretend,
pretend,
pretend in them?
(Do you pretend you love me in them?)
Tell me, do I breathe within your memories.
Tell me, do I stand a chance within your memories.
Tell me,
was I ever more
than temporary
in your memories.
Tell me how I live within your memories.

An Ocean Somewhere

I wanted to write these words down
before I forgot them;
I wanted you to read them
before you forgot me.
Here, I'm ready, I think I'm ready
to say –
there is an ocean somewhere
that sways and flows and rages,
and I am pulled and pushed
by its waves –
its salt is on my skin
in tracks running down my cheeks,
it wants to keep me,
it wants to toss me aside,
it wants
and it wants
and it's been centuries now
but it has not stopped wanting –
there is an ocean somewhere,
and if that is where you scattered us,
at least I know
we'll never
die.

Something Beautiful

There is something beautiful
in the way my heart looks
sitting in the palm of your hand.
The way it drips drips drips blood
into a splatter on the floor,
the way I want to pull up those tiles
and hang them on the wall
so everyone can see how much I loved you.
The way you don't quite know
what to do with it.
The way each of its pulses
makes you jump.
The way I already know
you're going to drop it.
(I already know, I already know.)
Maybe it's all the more beautiful
because I already know
you're going to drop it.

Silent

It is hard for me to love someone
who has a voice
but chooses to stay silent.

What Love Is

I don't think
you know
what love isn't
until
you know
what love is.

You Are the Story

You're in every story I tell,
at least in the way that I tell it,
at least in the way that I trail off because
I'm afraid of taking up too much space.

(At most, you are the story.)

(At most, you're the beginning
    and middle
        and end of it.)

Did I falter again?
I falter sometimes
because I've never gotten
this far.
Nobody's ever listened
this far.
Here's what I think:
I think that I'm probably
in love with you, still.
I think
that it may not
matter.

Imagine

Imagine you're floating.

(Imagine you've been floating for some time now.)

Imagine there's a rope, somewhere.
Tied to your feet,
to your waist,
to the tips of your fingers.
Imagine he holds the other end of it.
Reel me in,
you call,
you've called.

(You've been calling for some time now.)

Imagine he pretends he doesn't hear you.
Imagine he looks the other way.
Imagine,
imagine,
he drops
the rope.

(He dropped the rope.)

Imagine you've been floating for some time now.
Imagine you'll float forever.

Do you see,
do you see?

(Imagine you're me.)

Someone Else

It's all someone else now.

(Does that bother you?)

Someone else loves me.

Someone else
knows all
my secrets.

All of the quiet things
I'd never told anyone
but you.

I tell him now.

(Does that bother you?)

Truth be told —

(it bothers me.)

Your Name

Someday someone will ask,
and I'm still working on how I'll answer.
With a shrug,
with vagueries.
With the smile I've gotten so good at,
the one you'd never know was fake,
well –
(the one you alone might know was fake.)

Or will I say your name,
will I say your name.

Will I say
I've named the pieces
for each flight number –
the ones that took me to you
and the ones that took me away.

Will I say
I tried,
will I still be glad
I tried,
will I wish I'd tried
harder.

Will I say
I miss you.

Will I still
miss you.

Will I say your name.

Fools

I hate that you made us fools.
We were many things,
but never that.
Happy,
naïve,
a little drunk.
Sparks,
flickers,
fireworks.
We laughed a lot, remember?
And now I look back
and the moon is paper in the sky
and I can't recognize the song
that you're singing in my ear.
We're fools now, for all that we promised.
We're fools now, for thinking
we ever had a chance.

For You

I am for you.

Do you hear me,
do you hear me.

(I've always wondered if you hear me where you are.)

Not can, I know you can,
but I wonder if you do.

It doesn't matter.

I am for you,
whether you know it or feel it or want it
or not.

My heartbeats thud
like everybody else's,
but in each thud they say
your name.

And no matter
how hard I scrub,
if you dust me for fingerprints,
they're yours.

So if you ever feel
like the world is against you,
just remember –

I am for you.

Except, Perhaps

Nothing hurts me more
than the things you never said,

except, perhaps, for the things
that you said but never meant.

Razed

I've been razed before.
Rebuilt from floor to ceiling.
He stops by one day and says,
"I used to live here.
I'd love to see what you've done with the place."
And I am so often foolish,
I let him in.
I show him how I've been redone,
how the beams are sturdier,
how the foundation no longer caves.
But he,
he finds
every false wall,
all of the hidden rooms,
where I keep his laugh,
his fingertips,
his smile,
and a shot for shot remake
of the day he left me.
He watches it play,
I watch it with him.
(Though I have it memorized.)
And he turns to me
and smiles and says,
"It won't be like that again."

I've been razed before.

Rebuilt from floor to ceiling.

(But I am so often foolish.)

Look

Silence shouldn't have weight,
shouldn't have heft,
but look at these bruises on my chest.

Look how I'm buried,
buried,
buried in
the way you left.

Look how I'm flat on my back,
look how I can't stand up.

Look how I yell at anyone who tries
to help me up.

From here I can see every star in the sky,
from here I can count them,
I can count them.

Look how I count them.

(Each one another second you're not here.)

On a Beach

I think we're on a beach somewhere.

I think you're surfing
while I write,
while I glance up
from time to time
and look for you
in the waves.

I think you call for me,
you hold your hand out to me,
and I laugh and shake my head.

But then I think I put my pen down
and go to you.

I think I swim to you.

I think I love you.

(I know I loved you.)

But there, I think I still do.

At What Cost

At what cost, I should have asked.

At what cost will I love you.

My heart,
of course,
my heart.

It was a price I was willing to pay,
glad to pay,
hoped to pay.

I didn't expect
to pay with my dreams.

With my trust.

With a year,
a whole year in which
I cried myself to sleep.

With the shape of my smile,
the sound of my laugh.

At what cost, I should have asked.

And then,
had you told me,
I think I would have loved you
all the same.

The Latter

This idea of enough.

Of not enough.

The things we hold up to the light
and weigh,
and measure.

I do that less since you.

I am gentle with my failings,
with the staggering way that I want.

There are still things I wish I'd said,
but there's nothing I wish unsaid.

You said it was too much,
and I thought about that a long time.

Should a river be less of a river
if all that's there to catch it
is a cup?

Or should it roar.
Should it rage.
Should it flow
and flow
and flow.

I have opted for the latter.

A Hell of a Thing

My walls are covered
in pictures of what was.

What's been.

What will never be again.

I take them down every night,
I hang them up again every morning.

I can't stand the empty walls.

Everyone says empty
means the potential to be filled,
but all I see is empty.

It's a hell of a thing,
the way someone comes and fills
what you hadn't known was empty.

It's a hell of a thing,
the way they leave,
and now you can't forget it.

Your Heart

Tell me about your heart.

Does it howl at night like mine.

Do you listen to it.

Does it only ever beat,
or does it thud,
or does it pound.

Do you remember
where you got
that scar.

Do you remember
why you built
that wall.

Is it soft.

Is it stone.

Was any of it ever mine.

I Wonder

I wonder from time to time,
and I can never say for sure –

do I still love you

because you cracked me in two
in the best way at first,
in the way that let light in –

because you held my hand
like it was something more than
skin and bone –

because you outshine the sun
and at least half the moon
and a full three quarters of the stars –

(because you are you,)
(because you are you,)
(because you are you,)

or do I still love you

just because

I don't want to love somebody else.

Shine

Do you see the way
the world lights up for you?

(Or at least, at least
the way
I light up for you?)

If the tunnel is dark,
you always have me
and the way you light me.

At the end of it,
the beginning of it,
all the way through.

I promise to always shine for you.

(I can't promise to always shine.)

But I can promise to always shine for you.

What Good

What good are wings
when the sky's on fire.

What good are feet
when the ground is quicksand.

What good are hands
when they always let go.

What good are eyes
when they're never opened.

What good are words
if they're never meant.

What good is my heart
if he doesn't
want it.

What If It Doesn't Matter

What if it doesn't matter.
(It has to matter.)
But what if it doesn't.
What if the sun rises every morning
just because of the way the earth turns
and not because
we need another chance to get it right.
What if we believe
and we believe
and we believe
and it doesn't mean anything's
going to come true,
it just means
we're fools
with hands we've emptied
all our own
waiting
for someone else
to fill them.

And what if you don't come back.

What if

you don't

come back.

(What if it doesn't matter that I loved you.)

10:50

Is it ever like this for you?

Where it starts with something small,
like the feeling that my shoes
are on the wrong feet
and then maybe it's something a little more,
just a little more,
like it's raining in the house
and then I think my lungs
are in a straitjacket and
my heart is in a vise and
it's been night for one whole year and
I've only just realized the sun hasn't come back up,
that can't be good,
that can't be good
and
the clock still says 10:50
which is the time my flight left
the time I left you
no, no,
the time you left me
and everything's all wrong
all wrong
all wrong
and –

is it ever like this for you?

Backpack

A psychic once told me
I could go ahead and love you
but that you'd always be leaving.

He said you had a backpack on,
and you kept your heart inside of it.

He warned me not to let you
stick my heart in there, too,
but it's too late for that,

far too late for that,

I snuck it in there myself when you weren't looking.

Show it the open road, will you.
Show it the mountains,
show it freedom,
show it why I gave it to you in the first place.

Show it I wasn't wrong about you.

And someday, someday –

give it back.

Try

If it's meant to be, it will be.

I believe that.

But it doesn't mean

we don't still

have to try.

Hello, World

Pull me up by the roots, would you.

Love me for the way
I reach for the sky
even when
I'm cold,
even when
I'm empty.

Carve your initials
in my skin
as a reminder
for when you go.

Let them whisper for you,
let them sing for you –

Hello world,
I was here.

Hello, world,
I loved her.

Hello, world,
I left her.

Convince Me

He says, "Convince me,"
and oh I am so tired
of having to convince people
to stay.

Arms spread,
layers peeled,
look at me,
decide,
am I worth keeping.

Sometimes I say the wrong thing
and
sometimes I don't say anything at all
and
sometimes I get scared
and –

(am I worth keeping.)

"Convince me," he says.

It took me long enough

to convince.

myself.

Warm

Does it keep you warm.

You had reasons why you went,
and do they keep you warm.

Do they laugh against your skin
in the morning light.

Do they miss you when you're gone.

Do they love you,
do they love you.

Does any of it
keep
you warm.

My bed is six feet wide
and covered in blankets,
but I don't need a single one of them.

But then,

I'm the one

who tried.

All You Did

I have this whole world inside of me,
and you set one foot on its shores
and closed your eyes
and pulled a hurricane from the sea.

And you left.

(You left.)

You tell everyone you've been here,
but all you did
was see it from afar and break it.

You with your wanderer's feet
and your careless hands.

All you did was break it.

Does It

If a tree falls in the forest

and nobody is there to hear it,

does it make a sound?

If I love you

and you're not here to feel it,

does it matter?

Rivers and Tributaries

Read my palm –

I can't see anything in it anymore.

Just rivers and tributaries
that stop abruptly
and there are no answers
as to why.

There are never any answers as to why.

They all just curve,
they all just cave.

They all just spell his name.

Wishing

I wish on airplanes,
and not because I think they're stars.

Stars move me,
but not the way planes do,
the way planes did.

They don't carry hearts to and away.

And to and away.

And away and away and away.

And me on the ground, wishing

for to and to and to.

(To you.)

Autumn

Autumn is whispering in my ear,
and I keep begging it, "Not yet."
I loved you in the fall,
amidst dead and dying things
and biting cold I couldn't feel.
I haven't missed you in the summer.
(I've never loved you in the summer.)
Not yet, not yet, I beg,
but it will come,
and when it does,
I just have to remember –
that like you,
it will not stay.

What If

What if this was never what this was.

(What if I never knew you.)

Would I still know all of the words
to the pounding in my heart.

Would I dream other people's faces,
would I wake up reaching for other people's hands.

Tell me what I'd wish for.

Tell me how I would start a story
in any other way than
once upon a time,
he came back.

Once upon a time,
you came back.

(Tell me you remember.)

Once upon a time,
I loved you.

(Tell me how to stop.)

These Scars

I am fewer bandages now,
less dripping blood,
fewer fractures,
smaller holes.

They still ask me about you, though.

Have I seen you,
have I heard your voice,
have I missed you,
missed you,
missed you.

(I have missed you,
missed you,
missed you.)

But I smile.

I show them scars
instead of scabs.

They look sorry for the scars,
but I refuse their pity.

I fought for these scars,
I bled for these scars,
I tried for these scars.

I loved for these scars.

Drain

He thinks I'm a waterfall,
but I'm just a faucet
someone forgot
to turn off.

I don't flow,
I just pour.

You wanted part of me?
You have all of me.
I don't know any other way.

(You do.)

I wanted all of you
and I have none of you.

My fault, my fault –
I thought you were a reservoir
but you were just
a drain.

Someone I Used To Know

I didn't tell him who you are,
but he asked me about you.
I guess I say things in my sleep.
Did you know that about me?
Or did I not have anything to say
while I was with you?
Did I swallow my words even in sleep?
Did I choke on them?
Did I wake up sputtering while you slept
    on
       and on?

I ask him carefully what he means,
what I said.
What, that I loved you?
What, that I lost you?
What, that I'm riddled with bullet holes
and you poured silence into
each and every one of them
and didn't stop
until my own screams
were silent too?

He says I only said your name, though.
So all I have to tell him
is that you're someone I used to know.

Do You

I am never not trying
to fold myself into something
you can carry.

I file my edges so they can't tear
your pockets or your palms,
I shove cotton in my mouth
so I can't wake you up
with my screams,
I hold my breath
to be light as air
so you won't notice
the weight of me.

Do you love me yet.

I am soft
and quiet
and light.

Do you love me yet.

Over You

I'm so over you
so over you
so over being
under you
your thumb
your press
and waver
your certainty
about only
your uncertainty
the way you never
fought with me
or fought for me
or thought for one single second
that this is not for me
your I'm sorry
and I wish I could
so sorry
and I thought I might
and you're wonderful
you're wonderful
well nobody leaves wonderful
and I'm so over you
so over you
so over being
over you
so over being
not with you.

In This Way

I loved you in this way,
this way,
in precisely this way.
The way that buzzes,
that shivers,
that travels.
The way that holds.
The way that keeps.
The way I cannot shake,
I've tried to shake,
I don't know how to shake.
I loved you in this way,
this way and only this way,
a one-way kind of way,
a no turn arounds,
no detours,
no way out
kind of way.
I loved you in this way,
this way that weighs,
that weighs and weighs
me down and down
where it used
to lift
me up.
I loved you in this way.

And now I miss you in this way.

Favorite Things

I have a list of favorite things,
and my pen
keeps hovering
over your name.
I know I should cross it out,
but all I do is trace it.

I trace the lifts,
I trace the curves,
I trace your tilted smile,
your push and pull,
the way you made me laugh.
I trace the roll of your eyes,
our inside jokes,
I trace my pounding heart.

(I trace my pounding heart.)

You left, you know,
I know.
You left,
and still,
I trace
my pounding heart.

(I trace it in your hands.)

Listen

Listen –
I don't think love was supposed to be like this.
This balled up thing in the corner
that I stomp on,
that I hide,
that I muffle,
that I mute,
that I pretend,
look, I have gotten so good at pretending,
look, but don't look too closely,
don't look me in the eye,
don't ask,
don't ask,
don't ask about it,
don't ask about him –
this thing
that I pretend,
that I let everybody think,
is gone.

I don't think love was supposed to be like this.

It's just that
I did not know
what to do with it
when you did not want it.

Hollow

I've been devastated before.

What I mean to say is,
these bones are a vacation home
for hurt.

I chase it out,
but then they're hollow,
they echo,
they become tunnels
that lead nowhere.

I don't know which is worse.

I don't know why I thought
this time would be different.

Home

Home is where you are.

(I have not been home in years.)

Sometimes I think of all those flowers I planted
and wonder if you water them,
if you ever stop and look at them
and remember the girl
who flung seeds into the dirt
and said,
let's let them grow wild.

Do you dance in the kitchen with someone else now?

I am happy, you know.
I am happy,
which is not to say,
it's easy living
in a cardboard box
that leaks every time
it rains.

But every time it rains,
I think of those flowers,
and I hope
they're still growing
wild.

What It Is (Poem Within an "E")

I'm sorry,
I didn't think this through.

I lost hours of my day
and days of my month
and so much of who I am,
so much of who I was,
and it's fall, almost,
it's almost fall,
and I can't fathom how
I lost so much.

I miss you,
you know.
I know that you know.
I say it,
I shout it,
I know that you know.

I just wish this wasn't what it is.

I just wish this wasn't it.

Goodbye

The best parts of me are buried beneath my skin,
but you stopped digging
once you got past
my clothes.

And I asked you for more,
but to you more
always sounded like
too much.

I wonder how my words
managed to change so much
in the space between
my lips and your ears.

I'm not sure your words ever changed.
I'm not sure they came out
any differently than I heard them.

Goodbye
is always just
goodbye.

One Little Problem

Look, it's fixed,
good news,
it's fixed,
what a year it's been.

A hell, a hell,
a hell of a year,
a burning, dark
hell of a year.

But that's in the past,
that's all in the past,
it's better now,
it's fixed.

Look at it beat,
its cracks have sealed,
it's relearned how
to pound.

It's a brand new day,
and everything's great,
at long last,
everything's great.

There's only one little problem,
just the one little problem,
just the tiniest bit
of a problem –

(it healed with you still in it.)

A World

I just want to live in a world where
only gentle hands reach
and only kind words meet the air.

Where embraces don't suffocate
and questions aren't accusations.

Where I can close my eyes
and not have to fear
that the walls will cave in while I sleep.

I guess I can make it simpler than that.

I just want to live in a world where you still love me.

I just want to live in a world where you never stop.

Clean

You made my body into a weapon
I can neither recognize
nor wield.

So I hide it.

I cover the mirrors,
I cover myself.

I go out in rainstorms
while everyone rushes inside
with their umbrellas and their hoods pulled low.

I go out and spread my reaching arms
and arch my bowed back
and open my mouth in a silent scream,
no wait,
not silent,
no wait,
that's thunder,
no wait,
no wait,
it's me.

I go out
and beg the skies
to wash me,
wash me,
clean.

How to Hope (Poem Within an "A")

It turns out,
there isn't much difference
between everywhere or nowhere.

(It just comes down to you.)

I've been gone
for some time now,
for some time now,
you just wouldn't know it,
couldn't see it,
never open your eyes,
never open your eyes.

(I don't know how to close mine.)

But everything is dying now,
the wind's discovered how to bite.
Trees let go
so recklessly,
so thoughtlessly,
I beg them to show me how.

How to unclench my fists,
how to let things drop,
how to believe in spring's return.

How to hope, I guess.

I beg the dying trees
to show me how to hope.

Security Blanket

I'm not allowed to miss you anymore.

Like a child with a security blanket,
worn through,
covered in holes,
they keep pulling you away from me.

It'll never be what it was, they say.

Let go,
let go.

I agree,
I do,
but I tell them
they'll have to pry my fingers open themselves.
I tell them
I never did figure out
how to make this tongue form
goodbye.

I tell them
to keep you somewhere I can find you again
if I need you.

Late at night,
with reaching hands,
I think I'm going to
need you.

The Radio

I sing along to every song
on the radio while I drive and

I sing the words right,
I sing the words right,

except in my head
where they're all just your name,

except in my head,
where they're all just I love you,

except in my head,
where they're all just come back.

Constellations

We draw the lines
into constellations
to make connections that are not there.
We know they are not there,
but we want the pretty pictures,
we want the stories,
we want there to be
some reason we're down here
and they're up there,
some reason we huddle under blankets
and watch them fall,
some reason we bother them with our wishes.

I guess we just want it all to mean something.

I guess I just wanted us to mean something.

Before and After

He opens and closes his mouth so many times
I wonder if he's actually talking and I just can't hear it,
that my brain said no,
my heart said no, no,
save yourself,
this is the moment,
the dividing line
between before and after.
This is the moment.
And I want to stop it
like I want to stop a boulder
rolling down a hill
at the bottom of which
is my pounding heart.
This is the beat, beat, beat,
the beat, beat, beat,
the heartbeat before
a whole rest of my life of the after.

Island

We built an island,
the two of us together,
but I packed my bags and moved there,
and you used it as a vacation home.

(You used me as a vacation home.)

You leaned your worries against my bones
and your love against my skin,
like you were settling,
like you were staying,
but then you packed it all up
and left without a backward glance.

Again, again.

And me, on the shore, waving.
And me, on the shore, waiting.
And me,
and me,
and me –
on the shore,
wishing the tide would bring you back
wishing the tide would take me away.

Remember

I don't know,
I just think I could talk for hours to you
or listen for hours to you
or do nothing but sit on the phone for hours with
you,
listening as you breathe out and in.
Is that love,
tell me is that love,
tell me is any of this what I think it is,
what I thought it was,
what I hoped so hard it was.
Do you miss the sound of my voice.
Remember when you used to miss
the sound of my voice.
Remember when you looked me in the eye
in the middle of the night
and thought to yourself,
tomorrow I'll say goodbye.
Do you remember.
I only want you to remember.
You can do what you want from there.

Still

We are still those people,
and so,
we can never be strangers.
It gives me comfort, that.
Wherever we go,
however far apart we drift,
I will always be the girl
looking up at you in that alley,
and you will always be the boy
who kissed me.

Translations

When I ask you how the weather's there,
I mean do you ever miss me.

When I ask if you ever finished that book I sent,
I mean do you wish you'd stayed.

When I ask if you heard that song on the radio,
the one that reminded me of you,
I mean have you ever heard my voice
in a dream at night
and woken up reaching for me.

When I tell you goodbye,
I mean don't go again, don't go.

And if I cave and tell you
I can't live without you,
I mean I can,
    I just
        don't want to.

He Stays

I keep squinting in mirrors,
trying to see whatever it is
he says he sees,
trying to see past
all these walls,
trying to see through
all these cracks.
I keep waiting for my smile
to make it back up to my eyes.
Is this what he sees?
Empty shelves and sharp edges.
Is this what he wants?
I keep thinking it can't be.
But he calls me beautiful
and he calls me every morning.
He calls me wonderful
and he calls me every night.
He stays.
(He has more reason than you not to.)
But he stays.

We Can

I've got a hammer, nails,
duct tape, glue,
me standing here, ready to fix this,
and somewhere miles away, there's you.

I've got time, hope,
my heart in my hand,
me standing here, waiting,
and somewhere miles away, you telling me you can't.

But even if
    you can't,
        I still promise you
            we can.

Waves

I haunt this shipwreck,
but I'm no siren.
I sing nobody closer, no,
I howl them all away.

Stop trying to save me,
stop trying to save me.

I am a tempest,
didn't you know.
I storm, now.
I rage.

Sunshine got me nowhere.
Still water carries nothing,
changes nothing.

It was waves that carried you away,
and I'm convinced, I'm convinced –

it'll be waves that carry you back.

What If I Let It Go

What if I let it run wild,
rampant,
free.
What if I let it go.
It had a home
that didn't want it anymore,
that kicked it out,
that left it for dead.
It forgets it doesn't live there anymore.
It pulled for years, leash taut, collar tight.
It pulled there,
there,
only ever there.
But I've retrained it,
I've told it,
I've reminded it.
So what if I let it go now.
Older, wiser,
scarred and healed.
What if I let it go now.

(Will it go right back to you.)

If It Could

My shadow's growing longer.
I can't look at it without wondering
where your shadow is,
whose hand it's holding now.

The leaves are starting to fall.
I can't look at them without wondering
how they knew it was time to let go,
whether they tried at all to stay.

The morning breeze has begun to bite.
I can't feel it without wondering
whether I was always this cold,
whether I'll always be this cold.

The sun is setting earlier
and rising later,
and I want to hate it
for leaving me so often in the dark,
but I think that it would stay if it could.

I cannot say that for everything.

A Box in My Closet

There is a box
in my closet
that pounds.
There is a picture
inside of it.
A newspaper horoscope clipping.
Loose pages of a journal.
A dream I had one night
and meant to tell you.
My left hand, the one you held.
My right ear, the one you traced.
My laugh, the one you stole.
None of that
pounds, but –
(my heart, my heart)
(my whole heart.)
There is a box
in my closet
that pounds.

I don't think I'll ever open it.

Let Go

I think he tied a rope to the middle of me,
and some nights more than others,
from a thousand miles away,
he tugs on the end of it.
I hold tight to my bedsheets
and squeeze my eyes shut
and will morning to come,
will the sun to rise,
will him to stop pulling.
Will him to stop whispering my name
onto the exact breeze
that runs the length of the country
and slips in through my window
and tips into my ear.
Will him to stop feeding my hopes
whenever I'm not looking,
when I've left them for dead,
when they're finally, finally withering.

I will him to let go of that rope
because it's easier than admitting
that I'm the one
who cannot let go.

Wishes

I have no more wishes left for you.

I wished you here,
I wished you'd stay,
I wished you back,
I wished you well.

Now I wish
    my wishes
        for me.

Remember Me

I have been forgotten before,
but I have never felt it like this.

Like I blink,
and you forget my favorite song,
and I blink,
and you forget the color of my eyes.

Like I blink,
and you forget the sound of my laugh,
and I blink,
and you forget that you ever loved me.

Like seconds and minutes and hours
and days
and days
and days pass,
and I am less than I once was,
because you are not here
to remember me.

Alone

We're alone,
we're finally alone.

He's alone

    and I'm alone.

We got it wrong,
didn't we,
we got it all wrong.

We were supposed
    to be alone
        together.

Old Habits

Old habits die hard,
but tell me how to kill this one,
someone tell me how to kill it,
before it kills me,
it's killing me,
I think this time it might actually kill me.

You can't die of a broken heart.
You can't,
of course you can't,
of course you can,
your heart can't beat
when it's in pieces,
when it's not even in your chest anymore,
when he had it
and he broke it
and it's gone, gone, gone.

This is all to say
today was another day
and I survived it
but I do not yet know
if I consider that
a victory.

Open Your Eyes

I painted you a picture today,
but I didn't know how to make the sky
anything but black.
It's all I see now.
Black sky,
rain clouds,
someone forgot
to turn on the stars.

They say,
open your eyes,
I say,
no.

I don't want to know
that the sky is still blue,
still clear,
still starlit.

I don't want to know
that the darkness
is only
inside of me.

Shrapnel

He comes to me with shrapnel in his smile,
and I think how selfish, how selfish,
how selfish he is, this world is,
him for coming here like this,
the world for making him like this.
You think I want someone broken?
Well I do,
it turns out,
I do,
because I am broken,
and I won't fit right
against someone whole,
I'll pierce their skin and bruise their soul
and they will discover that I still carry
some of the shrapnel from his smile
tucked behind my tongue,
ready to be used
at the slightest push.

I'm sorry if I broke you,
I just wanted
us
to fit.

How Love Dies

I do not want it,
and I do not want
to be without it.
How can they both live within me.
Tell me how love ends
how love dies.
Is there a warning.
No sirens, no flashing lights,
but maybe one night
you sleep on your side of the bed
and I sleep on mine
and we are both too tired to reach.
Or maybe one night I stare at the ceiling
and you ask me what's wrong
and I say nothing
because I don't know, I don't know.
And you climb out of bed the next morning
and out of love by the next night
and I suddenly remember
what was wrong was that
I was afraid you'd someday
stop loving me.

What Does It Mean

I am made of butterflies and bonfires,
flutters and flutters and
heat.
I've been in love before.
This isn't that.
This doesn't hurt like love,
I don't cry like it's love,
it doesn't slip through my fingers like love.
This stays,
what does that mean,
what does it mean that it stays.

Flutters and flutters and
                              heat.

What does it mean that it stays.

Bulldozer

He carved his initials into my spine
just below mine
and now leaves don't grow here anymore.
Nothing grows here anymore.

Someone came with a bulldozer
and I kept waiting for him to chain himself to me,
but then I realized
he was the one driving it.

I guess I take up too much space.
I guess people are worried I'll fall
the next time it storms
and destroy everything around me.
I guess he's always wanted to yell timber,
always needed more kindling for his fire,
always wondered if something better might grow
here.

Or maybe he just saw something
he used to lean on
and didn't want to be reminded
that he used to need somewhere
to lean.

When You Go

My lips form the words,
but I don't say them.
They sit on my tongue,
pressed against my teeth,
pounding pounding pounding
against them.
I used to swallow them down,
but they're too big now,
too loud now,
they haunt me too well now.
You tell me about your day,
and I smile with closed lips
so they don't spill out.
You look at me,
and I look away,
so you can't see their shadow in my eyes.
Someday you'll go.
You know it, I know it.
I don't want these words
to be another thing
you take with you when you go.

Poetry

Poetry is love's leaves
where they fall onto the paper
after they've shriveled up
and died.

(Sometimes.)

And sometimes
it gets to be
the petals.

Phoenix

I do not know
what is supposed to rise
from all of these ashes,
but I suspect
it's going to be
me.

Our Blue Moon

What if that was it,
do you ever wonder if that was it.
Our chance,
our one in a million,
our blue moon
hole in one
scratch-off win.
The big one,
the best one,
the best we could do.
Did we do the best we could do.
Did we try,
did we really try,
did we look at each other,
did we really look at each other,
did we *see* each other.
Now that I can't see you anymore,
I can't help but wonder
if I ever really did.

The Things I Cannot Change

- the tide
- the seasons
- the way everything ends, everything goes
- the past
- your mind
- my heart
- the way my hands reach
- the way yours let go
- the past
- my mind
- your heart

California

Every other song I hear
is about California
and how the sun never stops shining there
and how everything's going to be better there.
I left my heart there.
I forgot to pack it with the rest of my things,
and you never sent it back,
and now I think it must be
lost in between your couch cushions
with all of the pennies and gum wrappers
that aren't worth anything to you either.
Everything's better in California, they sing.
It was, they're right, it was.
The trouble is,
I'm not there anymore.
The trouble is,
I'm never
    going
        back.

Someday

Someday the rain will fall up
and flowers will grow from the clouds
and stars will fall gently
into the palms of our hands
and you
    will love me
        again.

Not Yet

I always hope that
when you finally do turn back,
I'll be looking the other way.

What I'm trying to say is,
don't turn back yet.

What I'm trying to say is,
I'm not ready yet.

Let's Not Tell Them

Look at them,
look at them,
look how giddy they were,
how reckless they were,
how tightly they held on.
Let's not tell them where it goes.
Let's not tell them how it ends.
Let's not tell them that
    it wasn't
        tightly
            enough.

A Foot and a Half

Listen,
two steps forward
one step back
still counts
as moving on.

Two unwilling steps,
one desperate step.
Two reluctant steps,
one frantic step.

At this rate,
I will be lying on my deathbed,
and I will be a foot and a half
from over you.

You Will Leave

My heart has fault lines
built into its seams,
and you are nothing but tremors.
You keep moving me,
shifting me,
shaking me.
I hold on for dear life,
but whoever heard of
trying to hold onto an earthquake,
my fingers clutching soil,
cracks forming behind my eyes.

You will leave me rubble,
you know,
I know.

You
　　will leave
　　　　(me rubble.)

I Let Go

I let go of you every morning,
or I try.
Sometimes it takes all day,
like it used to,
like I didn't want to leave the bed
because you were so warm
and you made me so warm
and I didn't want
to let you go.
(This isn't that.)
Now I'm never warm,
I'm never warm,
whether I let you go or not.

Either way,
you're not here.

I can hold onto you,
and you're gone.

I can let you go,
    and you're just
        as gone.

Storm

I don't apologize for this.
I am clawing my way up,
clawing my way out,
and I don't apologize for this.
It catches me off guard, too.
When I smile and I mean it,
but suddenly a howl slips out,
lost and feral and I do not know where
I found it.
(Yes I do.)
(You gave it to me.)
I pull clouds across the sky
and hide behind them.
I cannot always be sunshine, don't you see.
You have
    to let me
        storm.

It Loves

I just don't think this is for me.
This moving on.
Thought about it,
tried it,
I just don't think it's for me.

You see these hands?
They hold on,
they don't let go.
They have blisters
in their palms,
and still
they don't let go.

You see these heels?
They dig in.
Push me,
go ahead and push me,
they dig in.

You see this heart?
It loves.

And it loves.

And it does not know how
to stop loving.

A Chance

Do you see me out there,
pretend you don't see me out there.
Every day, every day,
watering a rosebush
long dead, long dead,
nothing but dried branches
and brittle thorns,
like if I water it enough,
I can bring it back to life.
Pretend you don't see me out there,
staring at the branches
like if I look hard enough,
if I wait patiently enough,
if I hope hard enough,
petals will spring forth,
as pretty as the ones
that used to bloom there.
Pretend you don't see me out there,
okay,
pretend,
pretend.
So that I myself
can pretend a little longer
that there's a chance.

Nobody Tells You

Nobody tells you
when love lifts you up
that it will set you down somewhere
you don't recognize.
Somewhere far, far from home,
where all you can do is crawl,
and you breathe water instead of air,
and also,
and also,
you no longer have a heart.

Nobody tells you this,
or maybe,
    I guess,
        they do.

Maybe
    we just
        don't listen.

Ice

You'd look at me sometimes
like I walked on water
and it took me too long to realize
that the water was ice
and that it was cracking

beneath

my

feet.

Wide Berth

Did I get it all wrong.
I used to think my rib cage
was for keeping out
the reaching hands,
but now I think
it's for keeping in
my pounding heart.
Now I see why it's called a cage.
For its own protection,
for everyone else's protection.
Give it wide berth,
it lunges,
it claws.
It howls,
do you hear it howl,
do you hear it howl.
Do you hear it
                    whisper.
Sometimes it whispers,
but it's just a trap.
If you come close enough,
it won't ever
    let
        go.

Lost or Gone

I think he meant to move right through me,
but instead he moved me.
Zoom out,
can we zoom out,
can we please zoom out.
Someone show me the whys of this.
Why he picked me up
and set me down somewhere that
nobody else can find me.
I can't even find me.
Lost or gone,
lost or gone,
someone tell me
which
you are.
(Someone tell me which I am.)

Isn't It Cruel

If I had one hundred lives to live,
I would want to live
every one of them with you.

And isn't it cruel,
isn't it cruel,
that the only one I get –

I have to live
    without
        you.

Today

Today I am not
a river
or a tree
or a flood.
Not a flower
or a storm
or a star.
Today I am only
bones
and skin
and blood.
Today I am only
a girl
with a broken
heart.

Everything Hurts

Everything hurts.
I take a step
and hear the ground
beneath my feet
scream.

I freeze,
but standing still
only makes it scream
more loudly.

I try running,
feet as light
as I can make them,
but when I look back
I see
that there is ash
everywhere I touch.

Everywhere
anyone
touches.

It wasn't supposed
to be this way.
We weren't supposed
to live this way.
We weren't supposed
to die
this way.

Everything hurts,
and the world screams
and burns
beneath our feet,
and I wonder
how anyone can stand it,
but then,
I see –

they are all
   covering
      their ears.

Broke

You spent my love like it was currency,
and now I'm broke.
I can't seem to find a way to earn more,
to replenish my vaults,
to stand on my own two feet.
I keep asking for help.
Begging for it,
grasping at the paper edges of it
with desperate clenching fingers.
I had so much,
and I gave it away so freely,
and now, my pockets empty,
my heart empty,
I stand
on the corner
and I beg
for someone else
to love me so much
that I'll have
a little to spare.
(A little to spare for myself.)

Halloween

The only thing scary about today is
another month is ending
and you're
    still
        gone.

Your Ghost

Your ghost doesn't scare me.

I feel him just the same as I felt you,
a thousand miles away,
closest when my eyes are closed.

He is just as silent, just as sorry,
I can't touch him either.

The only difference
between you and him
is I do not think
he'll ever leave me.

Blame

I have spent long nights
walking back and forth
between our houses,
blame clenched tightly in my fists,
unsure upon whose doorstep
to lay it.

Here is what I have decided,
I have decided this:

It was my fault
for believing your words
instead of your actions.

It was your fault
   they never
      matched.

Here I Am

I come from stardust
and ashes
and people who love me.
(I try never to forget this.)
When the world drops
from beneath my feet,
I think of Cassiopeia on her throne,
I think of phoenixes rising,
I think of my mother and my father,
and their mothers and their fathers,
I think of magic and
all that was not promised
to any of us,
to any of us,
but here we are.

(And here I am.)

(Say It.)

I am scattered a little bit,
just a little bit everywhere,
did you see me in the sky last night,
I was there,
did you see me in your dreams last night,
I was there,
did you see me in a stranger last night,
I was there.

If I have to remember you,
you have to remember me.
I don't make the rules,
and in this, at least,
neither do you.

If you miss somebody, say it.

I miss you.

(Say it.)

I Could Not

I could not fall for less than this:

you.

I could not fall
   for less
      than you.

Nobody Can Tell

Nobody can tell.
I am still
five foot two,
my hair is still long,
still brown,
my eyes still crinkle
at the corners.
I still wear that grey sweater
most Sundays,
I still sit cross-legged,
I still prefer my nails
unpainted.
Nobody can tell,
it's all just the same,
nobody
    can
        tell.

(Because nobody can see inside.)

Isn't It Amazing

Let me tell you how wide it is,
let me tell you how deep it is.

Endless in both directions.

It is amazing how much I can hold.
It is amazing how much I can lose.
It is amazing,
it is amazing,
isn't it amazing

how much
it hurt
both to hold you
and
to lose you.

What Has Changed

What has changed,
can I tell you what has changed.

(Me.)

Somebody new
runs his fingertip up my arm,
and I don't shiver,
I don't flinch,
no,
I don't feel it.

This armor, it is thick, and
can I tell you what has changed.

(Me.)

Hey, you didn't want me
when I was me.

Do you want me now
    that I
        am not.

Two Years Ago

Two years ago someone built a sandcastle
and I said it was beautiful
while you said you'd seen better.

I think that sums us up.

I have said goodbye to you so many times
I don't think you think I mean it.

(I don't.)

The calendar tells me when I should miss you.
It says you once loved me on this day,
and maybe there's a chance
you'll love me on this day again.

(You won't.)

I just thought that we were beautiful.

You just thought
    you could
        do better.

I Keep My Heart Broken

I hold a pen in my hand
like a smoker trying to quit
chews on toothpicks.

I keep my hands busy
to keep them from reaching.

I write about you
to keep from writing to you.

I tell strangers I miss you
to keep from telling you I miss you.

I widen the cracks
in my broken heart
so I can dig around inside of it
for more
and more
and more words.

I keep my heart broken
   to try to get over
      the fact that you broke it.

My Demons

I feed my demons,
I sing them your name.

They claw at the backs of my eyelids
when I try to sleep,
but I don't mind,
I don't mind,
they're just carving in memories of you.

They say, remember when he loved you.
Remember, remember.
They say, remember when he left you.
Remember, remember.

I feed them so well,
they say no more, no more, we're full,
but I don't stop, no I don't stop.

I say, remind me when he loved me.
Remind me, remind me.
I say, remind me when he left me.
Remind me, remind me.

(I sharpen their claws for them.)

Lost

Like a child
whose hand slips free
of her mother's
in a crowded place,
and there are so many people,
everywhere, everywhere,
but she's too scared
to ask any of them
to save her.

I guess what I'm trying to say is I'm lost,
and I'm afraid
    I won't ever
        be found.

Who's to Say

Who's to say Sleeping Beauty
ever wanted to wake up.

What was she dreaming,
did anyone bother to ask
what she was dreaming.

I wonder if she misses those dreams now,
even though he says he loves her,
even though he says he saved her.

Maybe there was somewhere else
she wanted to be.

Maybe there was someone else
she wanted to be.

Maybe it's too late for her,
but it isn't
    too late
        for me.

Frankenstein

My left hand, your right.

My arm, your fingertips.

My head, your chin.

My hopes, your dreams.

This love has made monsters of us,
like Frankenstein in his laboratory,
fitting together bits and pieces,
trying to bring something to life.

(You brought me to life.)

You Will Think

You will think I'm looking at you,
and maybe I am,
but I
am seeing
him.

You will think I'm here,
and maybe I am,
but in my mind,
I'm somewhere
with him.

You will think I'm fine,
and maybe I am,
but mostly
I'm broken-
hearted.

Hello, Love

I love you like last November,
and the one before.
Do you remember.
(I keep forgetting to forget.)
It shows up like clockwork
every morning,
like it missed the call
that said
this appointment is canceled.
It shows up and it waits.
I call it in,
I can't help it.
I say, hello, love.

Hello, love.

I'm sorry to say
that he
    is still
        not here.

I Could Have

The only thing I know
with any certainty
is that I cannot possibly
love you this much
forever.

But oh,
    I could have.

Every Poem

What the hell was that for.

(What the hell was all of this for.)

I wrote you a poem.

It's this one,
it's the one before,
it's the one that I know will come after.

I wrote you every poem.

I emptied all of my love into your bones,
but I had nowhere to empty my heartbreak.

So I wrote you every poem.

Someday I'm sure I will run out of heartbreak.

But I once thought that
    about
        love.

Glass

He holds me like I
am glass and he
is a vise
that does not know
how not to tighten,
which is to say,
he holds me like he
is breaking me
and I am begging him
to shatter me instead.
I am begging begging begging
to be slivers,
to be shards.
But he lets go.
It's what he does.
He lets go,
and I shatter from the fall
instead of from his arms.

I thought he didn't want to break me.

But I think he just didn't
    want to be here
        when it happened.

Forever

I will get over
so many parts of this,
so many of the cracks
and crevices
and scars,
but I will never get over
the fact that you did not mean
forever
when you said you loved me,
but you meant
forever
when you said goodbye.

Surviving

Someone asked how I survived it,
and I said,
I haven't yet.
I walked your path with you
for so long,
and I am still trying
to find my way back to mine.
This part is unpaved,
uncharted,
compasses don't work in here.
I am still in the woods,
but sunlight is leaking
through the leaves,
it's not just dark all the time anymore.
I have not survived it,
no,
but I am every day
surviving it.

Miss Him While You Move

If you have to miss him,
miss him while you move.
While you walk.
While you run.
Toward, toward, toward.
Miss him while you move on.
While you try.
While you dream.
Don't stand still,
never stand still,
don't wait,
never wait.
Live, live, live.
Live without him.
It's okay to miss him.
But if you stand still
while you do it,
it
    will
        bury you.

What I Really Want to Say

I peel letters off of words
and words off of sentences
and sentences off of paragraphs
and paragraphs off of pages
and pages off of books
to strip it down
to what I really want to say.

What do I really want to say.

I really want to say
you move me.

I really want to say
I hope
    you never
        stop.

A Handful of Roses

A handful of roses
survived the first frost,
and I can't help but wonder
if they would have fought so hard to hold on
had they known
that it's only the beginning,
that it will only get worse from here,
that they have
    no chance
        at all.

Any of Us

I just don't want
any of you
to forget that
loneliness won't stay,
no,
you are too full to the brim for it,
no,
it needs space
that love
won't leave it
and
so much of you
is love.

I just don't want
   any of me
      to forget it either.

Come One, Come All

I open an exhibit,
I sell tickets,
no, I give them away for free.
Come one, come all.
Step right up and see
that crack there from when
he didn't call
and that crack there from when
he didn't visit
and that crack there from when
he wielded silence as a weapon
and oh, the grand finale,
the grand finale,
step right up and see
the way it broke in two
the night he said
he didn't love me.
Isn't it gruesome,
isn't it terrifying,
isn't it your nightmares
brought to life.
Come one, come all.
See all of the ways
    a heart
        can break.

I Just Wish

Tell me about
the night you hung
your fears on the moon
and let
me hold
your hand.
I use words
like brave
and words
like reckless
but what
do I know,
what
do I know,
less
and less
each morning.
I just wish
you hadn't
gone back
for them.
I just wish
   you'd let
      me love you.

Cold

You still feel like home to me.

It's just that home

never used

to feel

this

cold.

I Promise

What a tremendous sigh, it's like
you forgot to close
your windows and there's
a draft, a storm, a hurricane
inside
your soul
because
the world
is not
what you'd
been promised.
What
are any of us
promised.

I promise you I'll stay.

(Is that enough.)

(Am I enough.)

Happier

I am happier
more often
without you
than I was
with you,
it just never
reaches
    the same
        heights.

Hell If I Know

He asks me what love is,
and I say hell if I know.

Hell if I know.

I thought it was the way
you looked at me,
but now I think
it was only the way

I

looked at

you.

Sunk

The more I struggle,
the faster I sink,
but not you,
never you,
the moment you start to struggle,
you climb out and walk away.

I watch you go
    from the bottom of the sea.

I don't beg you to stop,
I let you go free –
I want someone who isn't afraid
to sink alongside me.

You and the Snow

You
and the snow
are beautiful,
I get lost
in the way
you glow.

You
and the snow
are cold,
I get frostbite
from holding on
too long.

You
and the snow
make me slip,
make me fall,
make it hard
for me
to get back up.

You
and the snow
are gone now.

Everyone swears
you'll both
be back.

(I hope you'll both be back.)

Kept

I kept the way you said my name.

I threw out most everything else,
but I could not part with that,
and I could not part with your arms around me,
and I will probably regret this later,
but I could not part with your laugh.

I swear, I swear,
I threw everything else away,
I threw
almost
everything else away.

(I kept the way I love you, too.)

(I have no idea how to part with that.)

Falling

I am falling,
I am falling,
I have fallen
fallen
fallen
for you,
are you feeling,
are you feeling,
do you feel
the same
way too.
We are holding,
we are holding,
we have held
on for
so long,
but now it's ending,
now it's ending,
now it's ended, or –

at least
   it has
      for you.

Can't

He says
he can't
keep doing this,
and I ask what,
thinking maybe it's
waking up early
and maybe it's
going to bed late
and maybe it's
eating pizza every day,
and I ask what
because I don't know,
I don't see,
I have no idea that
the thing
he can't keep doing
is loving me.

Language Barrier

You are a language
I am trying to learn,
but my tongue twists
around the words of you.
I sound them out,
I practice them
every morning,
every night,
all day in between.
I study and
I study and
I study you,
but still,
I'm like a foreigner here.

But still,
I don't understand you.

But still,
you don't understand me.

(Though, to be honest, you don't try.)

Crumbled

You can fix anything
that broke in pieces,
but nobody tells you
how to fix
the things that have simply
crumbled.
What can you rebuild from dust
from ash
from memories.

What can we rebuild from this.

No,
I know,
I've asked the question wrong.

What can
       I
         rebuild from this.

Call It

You call it surrendering,
I call it quitting.

You call it inevitable,
I call it impossible.

You call it for the best,
I call it the worst, the very worst.

You call it.

Time of death:
                        right now.

I keep pumping its chest,
I keep breathing into its mouth.

It's been eighteen months,
and I have not once
stopped
and let
love die.

So Much

You were never all I needed.

But you were so much
    of what
        I wanted.

I Think That's Why

I compare loving you
to carrying a backpack full of rocks
up every mountain
I ever wanted to climb.

I keep reminding myself
how badly I want this,
but you weigh me down,
you pull me backward.

You make me fall.

(I have fallen for you in better ways than this.)

I think
   that's why
      I carry you.

This Cold

I wear three layers,
but I still shake.
It's ice water in my veins,
it's snow down the back of my shirt,
it's you
    not loving me
       anymore.

This cold I cannot shake.

Strings

Just this once
I wish I'd given
my love
with strings
attached.

Maybe just
one string,
so I could
have held
onto the end
and pulled
it back
to me.

Because you
did not
want it.

And it does not seem
to know
the way
back home.

The Same Thing

Were we a dream
or just a lie.

(Are those the same thing.)

Sometimes I think about
all I had to do
to survive this,
and I wonder,
is this
what you had to do
to survive this.

I can forgive you if it is.

But can I forget you,
can I forget you,
please
can I forget you
the way
you had to
forget me.

(Yes, I think, yes.)

(A dream is just a lie.)

Monsters

I didn't realize
there was a different monster
under your side of the bed.

What did yours whisper in your ear.

Was it go,
was it run,
was it save yourself.

Mine whispered,
"He's going to leave."

I kept covering my ears,
I kept saying no.

But you listened to yours,
and the irony is,
that meant
      that mine
            was right.

He Guesses Wrong

I trace letters along
his spine with
my fingertips and
he guesses wrong,
he guesses wrong,
but I think
in the morning
he'll figure out that
all I ever wrote was
goodbye.

Stop

I turn the hourglass sideways.

I don't want time to go forward,
I don't want time to go backward,
I want time to freeze.

I want time to stop.

I want you to stop.

I want you to stay.

Right where you are,
one foot out the door,
looking back over your shoulder at me.

Stay,
and look at me,
and look at me,
and look at me.

Because once you go, you go.

Once you go, you can never
    not have
        gone.

I Wait

I cannot lean on you,
and so,
I lean on the door you closed.

(I wait for you to open it.)

(I wait to fall inside of it.)

(I wait
   to fall
      inside of you.)

(I wait for something that may never come.)

The Next Person

Sometimes when I picture
the next person who's gonna love me,
I accidentally picture you,
and I think no,
no,
he's why I have scars,
he's not why they're scars instead of scabs,
instead of gaping open wounds,
instead of a knife handle
sticking out of my heart.
He had no hand in the healing,
only the hurting,
and no,
no,
it's not gonna be him next time
or the time after
or any other time.
The next person who's gonna love me
is gonna have soft hands,
he's gonna use them to keep me together
instead of tearing me open.

He's gonna love me.

Loving
    doesn't mean
        leaving.

Something Happy

They want me to write something happy,
but I don't remember happy,
can't find it,
can't feel it.
They say try, honey,
try, honey,
try for something brighter,
something softer,
something less like
you've got holes punched in your lungs
and less like
water is seeping in
and less like
you're a sinking ship
with a flare gun
made of all the saddest words you know.
Okay, I say, I'll try,
I'll try,
someone bring me
a picture of us
or bring me
a memory of us
or bring me
him,
okay, and I'll try, I'll try,
I swear, I'll try,
just bring
    me
        him.

Again

I say again,
but I mean still.
It just sounds better this way,
this way,
where I say,
I'm sad again or
I miss him again or
the sun skipped my house
when it rose again
and everyone can just smile and say,
oh one of those days,
just one of those days,
and I can pretend
it's not every
    damn
        one
of these days,
and so I say again.

I say again,
but I mean still.

Someday I hope it stops
for long enough
that if it comes back
it will be again instead of still.

Always

It was you
　　　　then,

it is you
　　　now,

I have no reason
　　　　　　to believe

it won't be you
　　　　always.

I Still Do

You live in these words,
do you
feel
at home.
Do you
lose yourself
in all of the lines
and curves
and ways
you hurt me.
Have you settled into
being loved still
long after
you left.
Do you wake up
in the morning
and check
to see
if I
still miss you.
Are you disappointed
or relieved
every time you see
that I
    still
        do.

Because Of

How beautiful it is

   to be loved

      because of

         instead of

           in spite of.

Overflowing

I am sometimes more than I can hold.
I spill over with my wants and needs
and I think, I think,
it's no wonder you
couldn't hold me,
it's no wonder you
didn't want to try,
I am overflowing,
I am floodwaters
and high tides
and you couldn't swim
and I
refused
to be less.

I still refuse to be less.

Even on the days
I can't hold all of myself,
I know
that I am all
worth keeping.

Letting Go

How is it that
for you
letting go was as easy
as opening your hand,
just like that,
and for me,
I open
one finger
every month
and sometimes
I close my fist back up
and sometimes
I grab on
with my other hand too
and sometimes
and sometimes
and sometimes –

I just don't think
    I'm ever going to
        get over you.

In Miles

I measure it in miles.

This missing.

Some days it's a marathon,
some days it's a sprint.

Some days I sit halfway through it and I refuse,
I refuse,
you cannot make me.

Other days I'm like the wind
and you cannot stop me.

Nothing can stop me.

I cannot stop me.

Everything hurts,
my lungs collapse,
and I
    cannot
        stop me.

Or Maybe I Do

I don't know when my fingers
became claws
and my legs
became roots
and my heels
started digging
and my mouth
froze open
in this silent wail
and strangers
started plucking
at my heart
like it had petals
and they loved me
(they loved me not)
and they loved me
(they loved me not)
or maybe
or maybe
I do.

(I think it was when you left.)

I Stay

I stretch the muscle that stays,
and you work hard, you work so hard
to go.
I am toward
and you are away
and I am push
and you are pull
and I am in love with you
and you
and you
you work so hard to go.
(You go.)
And I,
I stay,
I stay
in love with you.

The Foundation

I see now I should not
have made you the foundation.

Perhaps a wall,
perhaps a staircase,
perhaps perhaps
a ceiling.

Something that can crumble
without the rest of me

coming

down

too.

Have You Seen Him

Have you seen him?

I used to mean it like
hell
have you seen
him
the way he looks
moves
smiles
hell
and now I mean
have you seen him
have you seen him,
please have you
seen him.

If you do can you tell him

I

would like

to see him.

Rewritten

You rewrote me from scratch,
edited me down to my bare bones,
peeled away my clothes and
skin and
hope and
now
I am naked,
stripped,
cold,
desperate,
I am desperate
for nouns and verbs and adjectives and
who I was when I
was covered in it all.
When I was everything
I spent so long becoming
before I became the girl
who loved you
and you became the reason
I'm not her
anymore.

We Drowned

The dam burst,
broke,
wasn't strong enough
to begin with.
What did we use to build it,
what didn't we use to build it.
What didn't we think we needed,
why didn't we think we needed it.
Why didn't we build it
higher
stronger
like our lives
depended on it.
(Like our love
depended on it.)

The dam burst
and we drowned.

You walked away,
I walked away.

But we
        drowned.

Dreams

Was that real life
or is this,
I cannot tell which
is the dream.

I was floating, flying, free
and now
I'm to my neck in quicksand.

Am I asleep,
am I still asleep,
someone
    please
        wake me.

Was I asleep,
was I asleep back then,
why
    did someone
        wake me.

Hell on the Heart

He was easy on the eyes and
hell on the heart and
buried in the bones and
all over all over the skin and
carved etched embedded in the mind and
forever going
forever going
I should have known
I should have known
because now
he's forever
                gone.

Sorry

You say sorry like
you found those five letters
in the bottom of your pockets
and you keep looking for more
but no,
it's all you've got.
You hand it to me like
you hope it's enough
but even if it isn't,
there isn't anything you can do.
You turn out your pockets and show me
like I care
like I should care
like I can still care
about your words or lack thereof.
Your silence
has always said far more to me
than your voice
    ever
        will.

Love

I tried to set it down,
but it stuck to my hands.
I carry it on my front
like a backpack worn the wrong way,
arms wrapped around it.
It isn't light,
no,
it isn't light.
Men with nice smiles come
and try to take it off of me,
but I bat their hands away
and curve my body around it.
I'm saving it.
I'm saving it for a rainy day.
I'm saving it for a rainy day
just like the rainy day
when you told me
you did not want it,
but maybe on this rainy day,
you will come back
and decide
you do.

(I'm saving it for you.)

Drunk

Me and love?
I think we met once,
but I was drunk
and I can't
be sure.

Tell me what it looked like.

Tell me what it felt like.

Tell me,
    was anyone else
        there
            with me.

Drowning

Oh
I am so used to anchors
I don't know a lifeboat
when I see it;
I just strap its chain to my ankle
and feel betrayed
when it takes me to shore
instead of sinking me.
I start clawing back toward the waves,
but there are no waves,
where did the waves go,
there's nothing but calm waters here.
Nothing to carry me out, away.

It's a good thing,
they all say.

They all say
it's a good thing.

They say there's no living in drowning.

I say
   there's no living
      without it.

I Don't Want to Go

I stay because of your smile.

That's it, I'll be honest.

It flips my stomach,
and I forget
that you lied about where you were last night.

Is forget the right word?

I choose not to remember.

Maybe that's the truth of it.

I stay because
              I
                 don't want
                         to go.

Do I Matter

My eyes are slow to open now.
I know what's there
and more importantly
I know what's not.
Tell me
did you see it coming.
Did you welcome it,
open arms, relief,
or did you run from it,
did you hide from it.
Did you fight it,
bare-knuckled,
like it mattered,
like I mattered,
did I matter.
Do I matter,
eyes closed,
moving through life
like a ghost.
Do I matter
    if I don't matter
        to you.

Still You

I no longer know
what the question is,
but I'm pretty sure
the answer is
still you.

Dead End

My mind is a maze

    and around every turn

is a dead end,

    which is to say,

around every turn

    is you.

My Words

He wants my words,
but I gave them all away.
I didn't sell them to the highest bidder either,
no,
I sold them to the guy
at the back of the room
who never raised his paddle.
(I sold them to you.)
Now he asks me questions
I used to have the answers to
and he waits so sweetly
for me to say something
say anything
say everything
but I lift a finger
and climb into the back of my mind
and dig and dig and dig
but all I ever find
are crumpled pieces of paper
with all of the words
you
    didn't
        want.

I Know a Lot of Things

I looked back.
I know I said I wouldn't,
I know I swore I wouldn't,
I know a lot of things,
it turns out,
a lot of things,
like did you know
that every star you see
is bigger and brighter than our sun
and did you know
that one day on Venus
is longer than one year on Earth
and did you know
that nobody
has ever made my name
sound like poetry

until

you

said it.

I know a lot of things.

But I still
    don't know why
        you're gone.

Mine

I call you mine in a growl
in a
don't you dare touch him
in a
don't you dare,
don't you dare,
claws out,
teeth bared,
and for once
nobody laughs,
nobody says
look at the kitten
trying to be a lion,
no,
everybody takes
a step back,
except you
you take a step forward
with a smile
that says
just as surely
just as fiercely
that if you
are mine,

I
  am
      yours.

What Might Come Out

Look,
I have opened these doors before,
and there's a reason I've closed them
locked them
barred them,
there's a reason I pretend no one's home.
I'm the house kids skip
on Halloween,
the one they run past,
the one someone made up a rumor about,
that they heard wails in the night
and so I must be haunted.

(I am haunted.)

It's not that I don't want you to come in.

It's just that it's been so long
that if I open up
I'm afraid of what might come out.

Where I Went

I left me when you did.
Tell me, was the weather nice where you went.
I went somewhere where it was dark
every hour of every day.
The air was thin,
I couldn't catch my breath,
and I could never seem to get warm.
I hated it there,
but I couldn't leave,
though most people called it
wouldn't.
And nobody visited me,
even though they'd try –
for some reason
they never got through.

(I was always just waiting for you.)

Not Anymore

You wouldn't recognize me,
eyes on the sky like this,
freedom in their shine like this,
you wouldn't know me,
couldn't claim to,
might finally really want to,
might call,
might call,
might call and say,
"Hey."

Might call and say,
"I miss you."

Might call and say,
"I'm sorry."

Me, I say, "Wrong number."

I am not her anymore.

Paper Snowflake

It turns out that if
you fold me in half,
you double me over,
you make me smaller than I am,
and it turns out that if then
you cut holes upon holes in me,
holes upon holes upon holes,
when I am finally reopened,
everyone thinks
I'm beautiful.

(Like something that fell from the sky.)

(Like something that's worth catching.)

Honestly, Honestly

Honestly, honestly,
have you ever seen anything like it,
have you ever
wanted
anything like it,
have you ever pushed pulled frayed
for less
for more
for anything else
for everything else
have you ever
thought you were made for
something else
something like
this
us

something

like

me.

(Honestly, honestly.)

(I have never seen anything like you.)

Anything That Goes

Somebody wired
my brain wrong
so I use my feet
instead of my hands
and my hands
instead of my feet
and I run
when I should hold on
and I hold on
when I should run
and I lean
did you know this about me
I lean
on things
that do not know how
to stay.

(And then I fall.)

Did you know this about me.

I fall
   for anything
      that goes.

Winter Solstice

The only thing different
about today
is that I have fewer hours
to miss you in the sunshine
and more
to miss you
in the dark.

In Silence

Flowers wilt
in the summer sun,
and me,
I wilt
in silence.

How Long

You ask when I'll let go,
when I'll give up,
and I say
I don't know,
I don't know.

How long does a fox
stay in the forest,
caught in a trap,
before it decides
to gnaw its own foot off.

How long before
it decides
its best chance
is to try and live
without a part of itself.

How long,
   how long,
      how long.

Until You

Later

I will

write a poem about it,

but for now,

I just want to say,

nobody has ever chosen

me

over a sky

full

of stars.

Cannot

It is less and less
that I

    won't

let you in
and more
that I

    cannot.

A Memory

Some days I feel just like a memory.

My laugh is an echo,
my hands just pass through
everything I want to hold.

I walk backward
only to walk forward again,
but never past where I've just been.

I'm here,
only ever here,
only ever here.

Wondering if this is how you remember me.

Wondering if
    you remember me
        at all.

Waiting

Sometimes love
is not
what wakes
you up.

Sometimes it's just
there waiting
for when
you do.

Promises

I have always been a fool for promises,
you see,
I believe them,
you see,
I dangle from the end of them
in places where the fall could kill me.
Have you ever wanted more than this.
(Than me.)
I have never wanted more than this.
(Than you.)
Look, I fell
and it didn't
kill me.

It doesn't mean I want
    to try it
        again.

For Me

I hope you don't think
I write any of this for you.

(I write it for me.)

And I Still Need You

I opened my mouth to tell you
I needed you
at the same time
you opened yours
to say goodbye.

But I still need you

to take it back,
take it back.

And I still need you

to come back,
come back.

And I still need you –

Glad

It is hard to know
you're out there somewhere.

But that doesn't mean
I'm not always glad
you are.

240

What You Fight For

You left your mark on me,
and I want it gone,
I want it gone,
(I panic every time it fades.)
Is this what you meant.
(This isn't what I meant.)
This, this,
what is this,
this razor-tipped love
that tears holes
in everything it touches.
(Is that why you didn't want it.)
Tell me what you fight for.
It isn't me,
it isn't this.

So tell me
    what the hell
        you fight for.

More Than This

At least twice a day
I decide I want to be more than this,
but then the night comes
and I forget
that I ever wanted to be
anything more than yours.

(It is hard to be yours when you're gone.)

Run

Look, I run, too.

You kidding me,
I was forged from
fight or flight
and I left my boxing gloves
at home.
So all I have are these wings,
all I have is this forward lean,
this push of a pull
telling me
to go.

I run, too.

(It's just that this time, I wanted to run to you.)

Love and I

Love wouldn't leave,
so I gave it a corner,
built some walls,
let it do its thing.

(Its thing is holding onto you.)

We leave each other alone, love and I.

I put one foot in front of the other,
and it sings your name
behind its walls.

I fall asleep each night
to its whispers,
to its wants,
and then and only then,
I think –

I'm glad it wouldn't leave.

Breadcrumbs

I drop breadcrumbs,
but not the kind
that will ever help
you find me.
No,
I drop the kind
you will follow
on the way
to realizing
you should
    have seen
        this coming.

Deep Breaths

I take deep breaths over you.
Like a rinse and spit
for my lungs,
like fresh air in
will cycle out all of the air
that burns
without you here,
like everything I inhale
that isn't you
will make me forget
there ever was a you,
that you
were the air
I used to breathe.

I take deep breaths over you.

And each exhale
                    is
                        a sigh.

Countdown

I count down from ten
where ten
is I don't need you
and nine
is I don't want you
and eight
is I don't miss you
and seven
is I'm forgetting you
and six
is I'm better off without you
and five
is I don't love you
and four
is I never loved you
and three
is I would have been a fool to ever love you
and two
is admitting that those are all lies
and one
is a deep breath
because it's coming, it's coming, it's here –
a brand new year
in which to try
to turn
them all into
truths.

Instead of Ours

I only wrote you the one poem,
but people framed it,
hung it on their walls,
it lives in their homes now.
We live in their homes now,
for that handful of minutes
when we were a we,
when we were hope
and possibility
and laughter.

Did you think it was magic.
I thought it was magic.

They think it's magic.

It's just that it's their love story now
      instead of
            ours.

Better

I have been made helpless by you
in better ways than this

and I have reached for you
with hands that shook
for better reasons than this

and I,
and I,
have always deserved

better

than

this.

But Mostly

Sometimes I turn over
memories in my head,
and I think,
I should have kissed you then,
and I should have touched you then,
and I should have held you more tightly then.

But mostly I turn over
one memory in my head,
and I think,
you shouldn't
    have left
        me then.

CONTENTS

ACKNOWLEDGMENTS

For everyone holding these words,
reading these words,
feeling these words.

Your support has been monumental.

I can never thank you enough.

ABOUT THE AUTHOR

Kristina Mahr devotes her days to numbers and her nights to words. She works full-time as an accountant in the suburbs of Chicago, where she lives with her two dogs and two cats, but her true passion is writing. In her spare time, she enjoys spending time with her family and friends, reading, and waking up at the crack of dawn every weekend to watch the Premier League.

You can find more information about her other poetry collection, *It's Only Words*, as well as her fiction novels on her website at:

www.kristinamahr.com

Made in the USA
San Bernardino, CA
16 November 2019